Acknowledgements

I would like to first thank my husband Clifton Lockhart. Thank you for loving me no matter what. You have played such a major irreplaceable role in my life. I don't know where I'd be if God hadn't used you to bring me back to Him. Thank you for choosing me even though my past said RUN. You honored me and made me your wife and for that I'm grateful and I love you.

I can't move on any further without acknowledging my two amazing children Ronald D and CJ. Each week you share me with people all over the world. I know sometimes it gets hard and I may miss a basketball game or two, but I work tremendously hard so that I can provide a lifestyle for you that I never had. I love to see you both happy and safe.

To Marita Kinney:
I know for a fact that God sent you to me. Thank you for your patience and assistance in helping me to get this book done. I really appreciate everything you have done for me. You have been a blessing to me and I pray that God returns it back to you 100 fold.

Last but definitely not least I want to take a moment and list a few names of some people that were influential in my growth and deliverance process.

Bishop Michael Brooks, Pastor Lisa Brooks (my mother), Elder Thomas Page (my Father), Prophet Todd Hall, Bishop Hezekiah Walker, Bishop J. C. Williams, Matt Ables, Shalae Madison, Denise Wiggins, and Dr. Nicole LaBeach.

AND THE WINNER IS...

Written by Tasha Page-Lockhart

Foreword by Marita Kinney

Dedication

I dedicate this book to my Grandmother, the late Shirley Ann Harris. She taught me how to pray until I felt the power of God! She loved me and I loved her so much.

I also dedicate this book to the late Apostle, Christopher Poole. He unlocked a desire for ministry in me. He helped me to see what was possible.

Copyright

© 2017 by Tasha Page-Lockhart.

All rights reserved. No part of this book may be reproduced, stored in a retrieval system or transmitted in any form or by any means without the prior written permission of the publishers, except by a reviewer who may quote brief passages in a review to be printed in a newspaper, magazine or journal.

All Scripture quotations, unless otherwise indicated, are taken from *The Holy Bible, New International Version®*, *NIV®*. Copyright © 1973, 1978, 1984, 2011 by Biblica, Inc.™ Used by permission of Zondervan. All rights reserved worldwide, www.zondervan.com. The "NIV" and "New International Version" are trademarks registered in the United States Patent and Trademark Office by Biblica, Inc.™

Buss, D. M. (1995) *The Evolution of Desire; Strategies of Human Mating*, Basic Books. All rights reserved.

ISBN: **978-1-943409-28-0**

Printed in the United States of America.

Table of Contents

Dedication 5

Copyright 6

Foreword 10

Introduction 13

Chapter One 15

Chapter Two 30

Chapter Three 33

Chapter Four 39

Chapter Five 45

Chapter Six 47

Chapter Seven 52

Chapter Eight 59

Chapter Nine 66

Chapter Ten 74

Chapter Eleven 78

Chapter Tweleve..90

Conclusion 95

About the Author 96

And the Winner Is...

Foreword

By Marita Kinney, BCC

Overcoming the struggles in life can appear to be impossible and extremely discouraging. Although you may feel defeated in some areas of your life, you can become victorious through Jesus Christ. Tasha Page-Lockhart is a perfect example of what it means to become a true winner in life. When I first met her at a conference that we both spoke at, I knew that we had something in common: pain. We were overcomers, with "a kindred spirit," as she likes to say. The anointing in her voice told an unspoken story. That story is shared in this book.

There are millions of women with layers of pain and adversity who are desperately trying to find hope as they peel away every layer. Tasha selflessly shares her testimony with boldness, giving her readers the encouragement to press forward no matter what they have experienced in life. God has a way of making her story believable to others, causing you to see what you've gone through.

And the Winner Is . . .

As she guides you through the most fragile times of her life, not to glorify her struggles but to take the power of silence away from the enemy, you'll begin to see God's hand all over her. Everyone wants to be anointed but no one wants to be crushed in order to get the oil. I commend Tasha for her transparency throughout her book. It was defiantly written with a purpose and passion. Allow this book to minister to your spirit and not be read through your carnal eyes.

There is nothing in your life that cannot be used for the glory of God. The word tells us in James 1:2 to count it all joy. Do you trust God with your darkest moments? Nothing that has happened in your life was in vain. He wants to mold you, shape you, and build you for His purpose. Yes! Even your pain has a purpose. It can destroy you or make you. You'll read how the trials in Tasha's life were used to make her. None of us would be who we are without the rough side of the mountain. Romans 8:28, "And we know that in all things God works for the good of those who love him, who have been called according to his purpose."

Greatness can be birthed out of pain. A lot like Tasha, I too had endured many hardships throughout my life. The more I tried to figure things out on my own, the more broken I became. I was addicted to pain and couldn't see myself living any

And the Winner Is...

other way. I'm so thankful that I serve a God that restores. He taught me how to turn my pain into hope for others. My unspoken walk in darkness came to an end through Jesus's blood that was shed for me. God's light began to shine through me. I became a best-selling author with over 35 published titles, sharing God's grace and mercy with the world. I too am a winner, and Tasha's book will allow you the opportunity to discover the winner inside of you.

Marita Kinney, BCC

www.MaritaKinney.com | @maritakinney

And the Winner Is . . .

Introduction

Hello reader! You have either purchased my book or borrowed it from someone—either way I thank you. Thank you for going on this journey of healing with me. God has a way of showing you things about yourself that you would never have seen on your own. I never thought I'd ever write a book, ever! I love to write music and sometimes as a teen I would write down my prayers but that's about it. I paused to cry about three times while working on this because I couldn't believe that I had survived it all. Some memories were so removed from my mind that until I began to dig deeply into my cloudy past, I could relive them again by writing this book. I couldn't believe that I had been such a terrible mother early on in my life. I guess that's why I spoil my children now—trying to make up for what was.

In the chapters to come, you will walk with me throughout my childhood, growing up in the COGIC church (The Church of God In Christ) and see what it was like having a gospel sensation as a mom. If someone were to ask me if I had a painful childhood, I would say NO. After reading the first few chapters, you may have a different opinion. I say that because, yes, like any family we had secrets. But through it all. my parents loved me and

And the Winner Is . . .

they did the best they could with what they had. They created so many amazing moments with me and my sisters that I often forgot about the other stuff until I was alone with just my thoughts and me. This is not a "tell all" book or a book to bash or defame anyone's character. I am only saying what God allows me to say in hopes that someone will be set free and encouraged.

As you read, I admonish you to lay aside your titles and positions and allow yourself to reflect on what life for you was, what life is now, and what you want your life to become. After you have done that, pray for strength, as I have, to make the necessary changes to your life that will please God. Feel free to pause and cry if that's what it takes to get it out. You may need to call and ask someone to forgive you or tell them that you forgive them. Hey, do whatever it takes to get to your happy place. Do what you have to do to WIN! That is the point of this book; it's not that I won a reality singing competition but that I won over the enemy. I won over myself, my insecurities, my own failures and mistakes. With the help of God, family and friends, I overcame drug addiction. I kicked a nasty habit of cigarette smoking, and I stopped living my life as a victim of molestation. If I can do it, then so can you! We are all winners. Let's walk.

And the Winner Is . . .

Chapter One

And The Winner Is . . .

It was around the end of February, 2013. I got a phone call from a family friend and he said, "Tasha, the Lord put it in my heart to send you to audition for *Sunday Best*." I immediately said, "No, I don't want to do it. I'm not into competitions." I was just totally against the whole idea of competitions, and a gospel competition show at that. I told him that I would pray about it and call him back with a final answer. What he didn't know was that before he called, I was in the middle of recording an audition video for a role in the Broadway production *Motown The Musical*. I wanted to play Gladys Knight, and so I had been studying one of her hits "Midnight Train to Georgia." I said a short prayer asking God what I should do about the *Sunday Best* audition and then immediately went back to preparing this Broadway audition video. Approximately 30 minutes after speaking with my friend, I received a text message from my cousin Monica Brown that read, "Hey, Cuz, I'm sending you the link to this website to find a song for an audition for *Sunday Best*. It's Your Time! "I couldn't believe it. I was lying across my

And the Winner Is . . .

bed and I looked up while laughing and said, "God are you serious? Okay, Okay. I get it; I'll go."

So then I instantly shifted gears. It was no longer about the Broadway production because apparently God had another plan and He had intervened. I started practicing one of the songs on the list, then thought to myself maybe I should call and discuss this with my husband and my mom. When I told my husband (Clifton) what I was thinking about doing, he started laughing and then said, "If God said do it, then I support you 100%." I didn't really know how to take that because the laughter threw me, but at least I had his support, so I took that. My mom, on the other hand, wasn't so supportive of the idea. She actually advised me not to go through with it only because she knows how political the music industry can be, and she didn't want me to get hurt. I totally understood where she was coming from but because I believed that this was what God wanted for my life, I decided to go for it. It is very rare that I go against my mom's counsel when it comes to music and ministry, but this I had to do for me.

I had been planning a birthday musical to be held at the church, The Rose of Sharon COGIC (Pastor Ronald Griffin) where I served as Music Director at the time. The musical was a major success. It was packed to capacity, and we had a life-changing

And the Winner Is . . .

encounter with God. I announced that I had decided to audition for BET Networks' *Sunday Best*. I was overtaken with emotion to see so many people rooting for me. It made me feel so confident to know that I had the support of my city. So the next day I flew to Houston, where I had a few days before the audition. Coincidentally, it was my birthday, so I went shopping and out to dinner with my "mother-in-love" who was living there at the time. We had such a great time, and the weather was just beautiful! I was soon reminded by a family friend what I was actually there for when she asked me to sing my audition song for her. I immediately got extremely nervous and almost changed my mind about going through with the auditions.

The morning had come for me to audition, and I was scared out of my mind. I'm always very nervous before I sing anywhere, but this time it was way worse than ever before. When I got there, I found a line outside leading into registration. Unfortunately, I had to wait but not as long as some of the others who had been there all night. I guess I arrived at the perfect time when the line was somewhat short. There was a ton of paperwork to fill out, and I was given a number, separated from Mom Lockhart, and directed to a waiting section. We were at a humongous church, and the whole scene was without question intimidating—to say the least. I kept thinking, "Why am I here, why am I

And the Winner Is...

here? There are tons of great singers here; I don't belong here." I purposely didn't go in name-dropping and telling people who my mother was. For those of you who don't know my mom, she is gospel recording artist Lisa Page-Brooks from the award winning all female group, Witness. I didn't use my mother's name to get special treatment. perks or favoritism. I went through the whole process like everyone else. After a long day and rounds of singing, I was given a "Yes" from all three judges and was one step closer to possibly making it on the show. A few weeks went by and they called me back to say that I was chosen as a contestant on "Season 6" of BET's *Sunday Best*. I was in total shock walking through the mall in tears. I started scrambling and pulling things together for my wardrobe.. My family and friends all came together and donated money and clothes to make sure I looked good on television. I have the most amazingly supportive family in the world.

(Page Family STAND UP!)

It was the day before I was scheduled to leave to film the show and Cliff and I received an urgent phone call from our First Lady and close friend, Natasha Poole. She asked us to come down to the hospital because our Pastor Apostle Christopher Poole (who was diagnosed with cancer a few months prior) wasn't doing well. We dropped

And the Winner Is . . .

everything to be by his side. The church was a little more than a year old and we only had a hand full of members. We were all good friends, and we all there at his bedside as he took his last breath. I will never forget that moment. Tears rolled down his face as he transitioned into Glory. I had to be strong for his wife and children, but when we hit the lobby, I lost it. When I told him I was going on the show he said that I would win and God would make me a household name. I couldn't believe I had to leave there and get my nails done to prepare to fly out for filming the very next day. I felt so bad for my nail tech because I cried the entire time he did my nails. I was devastated and at a loss for words. My husband and I had a rough patch in 2012 and Apostle Poole and Lady Poole were very instrumental in us working things out in a marriage. So as you can see, I had a really, really tough time even being in Atlanta for the show. I wasn't in the mindset of singing at all. I didn't even really want to be there. I couldn't go to the funeral. I was there alone without my husband and my children. I had no family there, so I was grieving on my own. I was in a very low place and honestly didn't see how I would make it through those next few weeks. I was totally depending on God to be my sanity and strength. During that time, I put myself on a prayer revival, which means I was praying every three hours. That was the only way I was able to make it. I was leaving meetings to pray, leaving rehearsals

And the Winner Is . . .

early to pray, and I had an alarm set to wake me twice throughout the night to pray. I prayed for three weeks, every three hours, while I was filming the show. At one point I wanted to be sent home; I even packed my clothes the night before a show. There was just a lot going on that the public had no clue about and a lot going on with me that only two people on the show knew about. Also, a few people were complaining because my mother was a gospel artist, saying the show was rigged and I should never have been allowed to audition. I was getting a lot of backlash there, but the whole time I had faith that what my mom had accomplished had nothing to do with me winning the audition. This was MY shot.

Well things didn't go the way I had foreseen. I made it all the way to the top two. As I traveled home, I couldn't believe what God had done for me. I wanted to stand on top of the tallest building in Detroit and tell the whole city the exciting news, but I was under contract and couldn't disclose any details about the show. Week after week we were having viewing parties. While this whole thing was going on, we lost our apartment due to black mold. Everybody in my family was sick and we didn't know why. My husband ended up finding out where the black mold was coming from. He opened up our utility closet where our heating and air conditioning system was, and it was full of black

And the Winner Is . . .

mold. We were trying to figure out why we were all sick, and that was why. We had to leave everything behind. We lost our apartment and had to move into a hotel. I was on television, millions of people were watching me and cheering me on and sending me Facebook messages, Instagram messages and Tweeting me not knowing that I was homeless at this point. Then we got kicked out of the hotel because one of the hotel managers was rude and disrespectful. I went down to the lobby, and I asked him why my card had been overcharged. (He didn't know that I was taping the conversation underneath the counter.) He told me he didn't need any help running his hotel and that he wanted me to go upstairs and get all of our things and leave immediately. We were already paid up for the week. I replied, "Well, why do we have to leave when we're already paid up?" He didn't want to hear that because he then called the police on us. The police came and I let them hear the conversation that I had recorded between the hotel manager and myself. The police didn't make us leave right away, but they were saying that he could have done an eviction and that we were going to eventually get put out. We ended up leaving the hotel later that day and going to another hotel up the street.

We stayed at that hotel for a week until we ran out of money. After that we went to my father-in-law's house.

And the Winner Is . . .

All four of us were living in a small attic. It was clean and we had our own bathroom up there. We put mattresses on the floor for the boys, and I slept in a twin bed that was already there. My husband slept in a white rocking chair. I would cry and pray everyday. And then when I thought things couldn't get any worse, they did. My husband was attacked and assaulted at gunpoint while our youngest son CJ sat in the backseat of our car screaming and I was a few feet away screaming and calling on Jesus. This was like I was the main character starring in a scary movie, where you know the writer won't let the girl get killed, but she keeps coming close to it. This was happening as the number of followers on Twitter, Instagram and Facebook were going up. More and more people were finding out about me. My songs from the show were on iTunes. As I traveled the country, people were inviting me to their churches to sing. We were still having viewing parties at different restaurants packed with people and they were cheering me on. Because I was going back to this situation, I was leaving these parties in tears by the time I got to the car. (Remember that nobody knew that I was in this situation.) I didn't want sympathy from anyone because I was trusting God and I just knew that if I stayed the course and I continued to trust Him, serve Him and remained faithful, something was going to break. I just knew it. I didn't know where it was going to come from. I

And the Winner Is . . .

didn't know whom it was going to come from. I just knew something was going to break.

Late one Wednesday evening, I got a phone call from a family friend who said, "I heard you were looking for a place to live. Well, my boyfriend and I are breaking up and neither one of us wanna stay in this house, so you can move in on Saturday if you want to." I said, "Okay." I hadn't even seen the house yet. I just said okay. So the next day we went there to see the house and when we walked in, all we could smell was marijuana. Come to find out they were growing it in the basement. The whole house was reeking of marijuana. Anybody knows that when you used to be a smoker, that's not a good environment for you to be in. Although we needed somewhere to stay, it was extremely hard due to the smell coming up the stairs. My children were asking about the fumes, "Momma, what's that?" It was just terrible. BET was coming to film my home for the show that week. The day BET arrived was the day I got the keys to the house. We hadn't done any renovations; we didn't have any furniture or appliances. All I had was keys to a house that smelled like "weed." I worked it out so that they didn't come inside; they just filmed us outside of the house. It all worked out. That was a tremendous blessing. The real miracle of getting the house was this. The lady that let us come live in this house did not own the house. I didn't know that

And the Winner Is . . .

until we got there. Once we started moving our things in, she told us that the house was in foreclosure. She said, "All you have to do is act like you're me. Write my name on the money order for the rent; mail it to the PO Box of the landlord. She'll never know it's you. She never comes here, so you guys can stay in this house and she'll never know. If she shows up, just say you're watching the house for me and you're my cousin."

She had this long elaborate plan, and I couldn't get mad because she was just trying to help me. I went along with the plan just to be able to get the keys. I got the keys and then once I got the keys I prayed and I said to myself, "Lord, I have to operate with integrity." I was ready to call the landlord and tell her the truth, so I called her and began to tell her everything that had happened. I told her the truth. I said, "You know I don't want to be squatting in your home. My friend allowed us to come stay here and I just want to be honest with you because if you ever showed up, I didn't want to lie." Especially with us being displaced all that time, I didn't want our family to be put out.. I wanted everything to be legit. I explained to the landlord, "I can afford to live here." I kind of threw the BET's *Sunday Best* name out there a little bit for some perks. I said, "I'm on a television show. I don't have anywhere to stay with my children. We moved into this home thinking that my friend owned it. When I found out

And the Winner Is . . .

that she didn't, I decided to reach out to you to see if we could lease it from you. You can run a background check or whatever it is you need to do." At first she was a little upset, but who could blame her. As the conversation went on, she was more upset and disappointed with the other person and was thanking me for telling her the truth. She showed up at the house a week later. She saw all the renovations that we had started doing, and she was just blown away at the work and the money that we had put into the house. She didn't even check our credit. We signed the lease that day.

It was such a weight lifted off of our shoulders, and it was all God.

Since then the blessings have been pouring in like crazy. We took our children to Disney World for Christmas—just able to do things that we'd never done before. This was our first home as a married couple. Our children had a backyard to play in. Because I won the BET's *Sunday Best*, I received a car, a 2014 Ford Fusion. I also got a record deal with Kirk Franklin on Fo Yo Soul/RCA. God has blessed us tremendously and I'm just grateful. I'm blown away by what God has done in our lives. In addition to winning BET's *Sunday Best*, my album came out August 5, 2014. I was nominated for four Stellar Awards and I ended up coming home with one, New Artist of the Year. My album was released

And the Winner Is...

in stores and online everywhere. We taped the Stellar Awards March 28, 2015. It aired on Easter Sunday after the awards in 2015. To have an album that wasn't even a year old at the time, to be nominated in four categories and to be able to perform after the awards was a dream come true that doesn't often happen to new artists.

It was clearly the hand of God in my life.

I've been blessed to be on *106 & Park*, which is not even a gospel platform. It's a major secular platform for youth. I was on *106 & Park*, right before they discontinued the television show. Now they just do a web series online. I was able to be in *Jet Magazine*. I was featured on *Essence* online magazine. I was on *Celebration of Gospel*. I was on *Bobby Jones Gospel*. I've sung at the *BMI Trailblazers Award* 2014, 2015, and 2016. God is just amazing. He just keeps blowing my mind. I've toured with McDonalds, House of Blues/Live Nation, and Tyler Perry (*Madea on the Run*). My phone rings daily with opportunities that I know could only have come from God. I'm so grateful for what He is doing in my life. I was blessed to have the lead role in a movie called *Who Can I Run To* written and produced by Paul Hannah. I was looking over my script and when I got there they said, "Mrs. Lockhart, here's your trailer. You're the lead actress. This is a movie." I was so terrified. I had never been in a movie before.

And the Winner Is . . .

I was acting alongside Antoine Tanner from *One Tree Hill*, Cherie Johnson from *Family Matters*, Lil' Mo, *My Boy Major*, Trisha Mann, Marvin Sapp, Jessica Reedy and Kel Mitchell. I had had no professional training as an actress prior to the movie, but they trusted me and put big money into the production. It was just another humbling experience.

I told somebody, "God has really shown me how much He really loves me." God has done tons of things for me, but just over the past three years, I can see how He has raised me up and put me in front of millions of people. I get to sing, travel and minister to thousands of people on a weekly basis. It really shows me how much He loves me in spite of all my failures. Every time I walked away from Him, every time I disappointed Him, every time I wasn't faithful, He remained at my side. He's proven Himself to me over and over and over again. So that brings me to where I am now, touring the world singing, preaching, spreading the message of Jesus Christ, writing books, and hosting my annual PK United Conference (Preachers Kid United). It's funny how people think I just appeared on the scene but really I've been grinding and putting in work for years. I also have an amazing team of people working hard pushing and praying for me, along with an extremely supportive and incredible husband who works with me and holds down the

And the Winner Is . . .

home front when I'm away. One of the hardest parts about my job is being away from my husband and children. I miss seminal moments in their lives all the time and it always seem like the children have grown an extra inch when I return. But at the end of the day, it's all about God's divine timing. When He decides that you're ready, don't waste time like I did. Start getting ready now!

> *Lord deliver us from the* **SPIRIT OF INERTIA.** *(A tendency to do nothing* **OR TO REMAIN UNCHANGED)**
>
> **@TASHAPAGELOCKHART**

Chapter Two

High Hopes

I grew up on the west side of Detroit, Michigan. I was a very bright kid. My personality was loving, bubbly, and I always wanted to have fun. Of course, I loved to sing. My sisters and I had a group called The Page Sisters. There were three of us by the same mom and dad. As you know, my mom is a singer and back then my dad played drums. He is a preacher now and runs a heating and cooling business. My sisters and I are two years apart, stair step. I'm the oldest and I think we started the group when we were three, five and seven. We would go around to different churches and sing. We did all the outside festivals and traveled out of town to Ohio and other surrounding areas. My mom took us on the road a few times to sing with her and we were the spokespersons for the Children Helping Children organization. My dad had us involved in so many activities like showcases and talent shows. I started doing voice overs and jingles for major corporations such as Bisquick, United Way, Dodge Caravan, Chrysler, Kmart, the Detroit Red Wings. That's just a few. I did that between the ages of seven and fourteen. I was getting checks as a kid for $10,000. God was truly blessing me even at a young

And the Winner Is . . .

age. Ironically, my stepfather, whom my mom later remarried, is Michael Brooks from the male group Commissioned. He was the first person ever to take me into the studio to record.

Through my mom and him, I got the opportunity to do the jingles. They would already be at the studio recording her group Witness because he was also a producer. We would be there as kids running around and playing.. They would say, "Okay, we need a kid's voice." I was always up there so they said, "Come on Tasha." They put me in the booth and the rest is history. I've been doing this for a long time.

I was a straight "A" student and I learned very quickly. All throughout my elementary school years I did talent shows, I sang at school, and I was in the gospel choir. I also was a cheerleader, played volleyball, and basketball all throughout grade school and junior high. However, in middle school and high school, basketball was my favorite sport.. Good grades, basketball team, student council, and I led the gospel choir. I would sing the national anthem and then suit up to play in the game. Scouts from different colleges came to see my team play. My family was just very excited, and everybody was rooting for me. At the time I was also winning solo and ensemble competitions for my chorus class. I won four blue (first place) medals. I would sing in

And the Winner Is...

French, Spanish and Italian. I was also picked to be one of the top singers in our region to record a CD in the Region C Concert Choir. All of these things were going on and from the outside looking in, it looked like I was going to be something great. My English teacher even told my mother, "If Tasha just stays focused, she could possibly be a journalist one day," because I was so good in English. Everybody had high hopes for me. Everyone, but me.

And the Winner Is . . .

Chapter Three

The Perfect Childhood

Growing up as a kid, we were very sheltered. We grew up in a Christian home and were part of the C.O.G.I.C. church, The Church of God In Christ. We couldn't wear pants, we weren't allowed to go to the movies and my parents didn't really like us visiting other churches of different denominations. We couldn't wear makeup or earrings. They were really, really, really strict on those types of things. They used to say, "If you don't do right, you're going to go to hell. If you tell lies, you're going to go to hell. If you kiss a boy, you're going to get pregnant and you're going to go to hell." Everything was, if you do this, you're going to go to hell, so we grew up hell scared. It wasn't until I started going through such rough situations that I really got to know Jesus Christ for myself and develop a true relationship with Him. Now I'm not serving Him because I'm hell scared. I'm serving Him because I really love Him and He's been good to me.

Praise break right here!!!!!

Ok, now back to my childhood. I had to sneak and listen to R&B music. I can remember sitting on the

And the Winner Is . . .

floor of my dad's basement and listening to Nas, Whitney Houston and D'Angelo. We had a huge surround sound stereo system with a cassette player and a five-CD changer. I would put my headphones on and listen to Missy Elliot, Kelly Price, Tweet, Faith Evans, and Biggie—just to name a few. I would try so hard not to sing the songs out loud but sometimes I just couldn't hold it in. The music would sound so good to me that I would start dancing around and singing at the top of my lungs. Then I would get caught. My dad would come downstairs, take my CDs and tapes and throw them out. I would get so mad I would cry, but I knew my dad was just looking out for me and that he loved me. I was still mad though.

Growing up in the COGIC church, we attended all of the jurisdictional meetings. Again, my sisters and I had a group, so we sang together there. We sang at everything. They changed our name at that time from The Page Sisters to Page Three. As a child I never heard my mother curse or my parents argue. I never saw them drink. I also never saw them smoke. I never witnessed them do anything other than show me characteristics of Jesus Christ. In my mind if someone were to ask me, "Did you have a rough childhood?" I would have to say that no, I didn't have a rough childhood. But while all of this was going on and I appeared to be having the perfect childhood, I was really suffering inside.

And the Winner Is . . .

Suffering occurred inside because from the age of seven-years old until roughly age eleven, I was being molested by four people. Some of my offenders were family, and even close friends of the family. A lot of inappropriate activity went on. Touching in my private area. Touching, making me do things to them. Just very inappropriate sexual activity. At one point we were over at a family friend's house. My father was upstairs and I was downstairs in the basement being mishandled by his friend. He would pull me around the corner and would put his tongue down my throat. I was only nine-years old. I was afraid to say anything. I didn't want to get in trouble. I didn't want to get punished or get a whooping. I didn't want to be looked at as the nasty girl.

Again, remember, my family had high hopes for me. I had great grades and had good stuff going on for me. I couldn't mess that up by telling what was really going on. Even though I didn't like it and didn't feel good about it, I felt nasty. I remember being so afraid. One of the individuals who molested me was one of my uncles. He was also abusing his wife, which intensified my fear. I didn't have the courage to tell him no. I didn't know if he was going to hurt me too. I was also afraid he and my father would have gotten into a fight and that he would do something awful to my dad. I didn't want to be the one to break up the family. I didn't want

And the Winner Is . . .

my grandmother to be disappointed in me. I just didn't want to cause any trouble.

Therefore, I remained silent. I never said anything until now. I'm 33-years old and I'm just now really vocalizing this. I truly believe that this is something that has gone on in my family before. Family secrets can destroy lives. Generational curses keep going because they have been kept secret. If my father would have come to me, if somebody in my family would have come to me and said, "Tasha, this is what to look for. This is not supposed to happen to you. Don't let anyone touch you like this. I don't care if they're a family member or this is what has gone on in our family before. watch out for this," I would have been warned. Instead they wanted to keep it a secret. I didn't know what to watch out for. I didn't know that this was wrong. In my mind, every young girl at my school was going through this. Molestation became my new normal. I did not know that the other girls weren't going through that also. Not to mention that I was already over-developed. I was the only fourth grader at my school wearing a bra. I was miserable inside. On the outside, I looked like I had the perfect childhood. I was smiling, singing, I had good grades, and all of this great stuff going on. But I was miserable inside and I couldn't tell anyone.

And the Winner Is . . .

Going into my teenage years, my parents divorced. It was a rough time for my sisters and me because all we knew was Mom and Dad. We also didn't know until we got older that we were basically almost poor. We didn't know that we had eviction notices, their cars were being repossessed, and lights and gas were being shut off. We didn't know any of this. My mother and my father did an amazing job at covering us as children and not allowing what was going on to affect us growing up and having a good childhood. We had no idea that we were suffering or that we were struggling. When my parents divorced, my mother didn't sit us down and say, "Your father and I are getting divorced." One day Daddy wasn't living with us anymore. We went from having a family life to staying with one parent during the week and the other only on weekends. Soon after that my mom's music career started picking up and she was gone a lot. We spent time with family members here and there. We were always with a different sitter. One thing I can say about my mom is that she made sure the sitters came to our house so we could be comfortable at home. We would cry all the time though because we wanted our mother, but we really wanted our parents together. My dad was trying to work and so was my mom. They both needed help. We lived with several family members, and we just never really had a place of our own once they divorced. I remember we had to appear in court to say whom

And the Winner Is . . .

we wanted to live with, in front of the other parent. I had the toughest time with that. It was so tough to choose because I loved my mom so much; she was my mother; she had given birth to me. I had a special love for her. I was in awe of her ability to sing and I still wanted to stay with my mom, but she was gone all the time. The only person I saw often was my dad. Therefore, I chose my dad. Oh, and we were told on the ride over there by him and my aunt to choose him. I knew that had to have hurt my mom. It just put us in a bad place. I don't think any child should ever have to go through that. It was a tough time in my life.

And the Winner Is . . .

Chapter Four

Be Right Back Mom

If someone tells you they'll be right back, you actually expect them to come right back, right? If someone tells you they're going to the store up the street, you expect them to go to the store and come back. If someone tells you they're going to wash a load of clothes, you expect them to be gone maybe five to ten minutes depending on how you sort your clothes. You expect them to do exactly that and then come right back. Especially if this person is a minor and you're trusting them slowly with responsibility. If they're driving your vehicle or those types of things, you expect them to do what you said and then you expect them to come back. Well, at age 14, my mom remarried. It was a tough transition for me because we went from calling my stepfather Mr. Brooks to, in a day, Dad. We had to get used to it. He's been an amazing father, but it was a tough transition because all I knew my whole life as our dad was Thomas Page. I can recall when my mom took us to Ruby Tuesdays, a restaurant. We sat down, and his two children were there also. We sat across the table from each other and had dinner with them. We grew up with his children, so they

And the Winner Is...

were our friends. We all went to the same church. So when we arrived at the restaurant initially we said, "Hey, what's up, y'all?" It was nothing unusual. They sat down and my mom says, "So, we have an announcement to make. We're married." It was like we had seen a ghost. I went from looking across the table at my friend to, oh my God, you're my sister now. Oh my God, you're my brother now. Nobody said anything. We just looked puzzled. "What?" However, that was not the only surprise. My mother then said, "We're getting ready to start a church." I freaked out because I instantly became someone's stepdaughter and a preacher's kid too. It was a very weird, awkward transition for me, to go from just being a regular kid who just liked church to a kid that everybody was watching. It was a lot of pressure transitioning from just being regular old Tasha, to now Tasha, the PK.

If you know anything about rebellion, you know that once rebellion sets in, there are a lot of doors that will open. I had already started smoking at 12-years old. My mom caught me on the side of our apartment building. I think I was smoking a black and mild. I began skipping school in middle school but was still getting good grades. My behavior shifted after my parents divorced and got worse after my mother re-married. It was all just acting out because of the changes. It was also due to the fact that nobody knew about the molestation. I became

And the Winner Is . . .

very promiscuous during that time because that's the door that had been opened in my life. I had already developed an appetite for sex at seven-years old. I was a little different than some of the girls that you see walking around. I had seen some stuff and done some stuff. And a lot of things had been done to me. I wasn't your typical 14-year old teenager. I was very experienced at that point.

I was considered the fast girl. I was considered the girl who was always on a man's lap. Always in a man's face. I did not know why I was like this. I did not understand the behavior until I became an adult. I would be so angry with myself after I would do certain things like flirting with grown men. I would hate myself for this. I couldn't stop doing it though. I craved attention from men. I craved it from boys at school, from teachers. Any guy that would look at me in the slightest little way, I craved it. It was terrible. I just began to rebel more and more. Then the time came where I started stealing. I was stealing clothes and selling them. I was just bad!

We lived on the 19th floor. I would tell my mother, "Mom, I'm going downstairs to wash a load of clothes." Two weeks would go by and my mother wouldn't see me. I would be in the streets. I would be at this guy's house, this friend's house. I would just be out there. I would ask if I could go to the

And the Winner Is...

store that was located in the basement of our apartment building and then disappear for days at a time. This kept happening and happening. I would leave for school on a Friday and say, "I'm going to spend the night at Kyra's house. I'm going to spend the night at Bridget's house." I wasn't really going to Bridget's house or to Kyra's house. I was going to see my boyfriend. I was spending the weekend with this dude at 14- and 15-years old, and of course we were having sex.

I remember the day when my mom walked in as I was lying on the floor in the living room crying. I said, "Mom, I have to tell you something." She said, "What? You've been having sex?" She already knew. She said, "I was praying, and the Holy Spirit revealed to me that you had been having sex." There's a twofold thing here where it's a blessing to have a mother that prays, but also, you can't hide anything from a mother who prays. My mother always found out all my schemes, all my tricks, all the stuff I was doing. Everything I was doing. She always knew, and she didn't even tell me she knew. She just prayed. All along I was having sex with grown men, doing sexual stuff at school in the bathroom and just out of control. One thing led to another and when you keep opening those doors, the enemy has a field day. When you crack it, he's going to bust that door wide open. You cannot play with this kind of stuff. You can't play with the

And the Winner Is...

enemy because he is not playing with you. His job is to kill, steal and destroy.

Now as an adult, I pray for my children. I lay hands on them in the middle of the night. I pray against the spirit of curiosity because I wasn't raised like that. I wasn't raised to smoke. I wasn't raised to drink. I wasn't raised to do a lot of the stuff that I did. It was a spirit of curiosity in me that led me to try those things. I just had to see what it was like. My mother used to always tell me, "Tasha, experience is not always the best teacher. Information is."

Just listen to me. I can tell you what I went through to prevent you from going down the road I went down. That advice is the main reason for writing this book—to save someone's life, to prevent someone from going down the road that I went down.

And the Winner Is . . .

> EVEN WHEN I'M IN THE VALLEY I'M STILL ON THE MOUNTAIN.
>
> @TASHAPAGELOCKHART

Tasha Page-Lockhart

Chapter Five

Who Am I?

Who am I? I had to ask myself that question, who am I? Because growing up in high school, I played basketball. I was really good at a few sports but especially basketball. I absolutely loved playing basketball. There was a culture to that sport and a group of people who surrounded me. The girls at my high school were hard, and some of them were lesbians. Some of them I knew were and others I later found out were also. The sexual appetite that was in me over the years really was a spirit of perversion. That was the root of it. Again, I was curious. I started looking at girls and dressing a certain way. I started wearing basketball shorts, tank tops, gym shoes, and breakaway pants on days when I didn't have games. I went from being a girly girl, wearing skirts, purses, makeup and all of that to hair in a ponytail, braids, and basketball shorts. Those were red flags immediately. My mother saw it. She said something to me about it.

Parents, you have to notice these red flags. It's our job as parents to see it before it has fully manifested. Because I honestly believe if my mother hadn't stepped in and counteracted what the enemy was

And the Winner Is . . .

trying to do in me, I would have been a lesbian to this day.

Let me back up a little though. During this time, we had a babysitter and my parents did not know that she was a lesbian. She exposed me to so many things from gay clubs where I saw men dressed up as women, women dressed as men. I was getting it from school and home. My parents trusted this person to take care of me, and the whole time they didn't know about what she was doing. At that point, I was not going to tell them because I had all this stuff working in me, this curiosity and rebellion. In my mind, I had something up on my traveling parents. I was thinking that I was getting back at them by keeping this secret. Another trick of the enemy. It just exposed me to a lot until my mother began to pray and was led by the Spirit to shut the whole thing down. As an adult, that fascination with women still lingered around, but it never fully manifested. I never had a serious relationship with a woman but I might have. I almost lost my identity.

Thank you Jesus and thank you Mom!

And the Winner Is . . .

Chapter Six

Two Packs a Day

At this point, my life was in a downward spiral. I was declining every day. I was feeling like I was gonna lose my mind. One thing led to another. Never say what you're not going to do. I said out of my mouth, "I'll never smoke weed, I'll never drink, I'll never pop pills. I'll never do this and I'll never snort cocaine." But I found myself doing all the things I said I would never do. It was a generational curse that skipped my parents. Both of my grandfathers were into drugs and alcohol. Again, I did not know any of this. Family secrets are what led to my bondage.

You have to expose it. You have to tell your children what's going on in your bloodline. You have to make the devil the liar he is. You have to tell your children what's going on and tell them the truth. Even tell them some of your personal stories. Yes, you must tell them. I share certain things with my children on the level that they can understand. The older they get, the more I reveal to them. I don't want them to have to hear it from anyone else. I tell them myself. I want them to know what to look for.

And the Winner Is...

I started smoking weed every day. I would steal change out of my mother's change receptacle, handfuls of it. I would take money out of people's pockets. I would steal money out of people's purses to buy drugs. It got that bad. I started stealing clothes from the mall and selling them. I would steal perfume testers from the department stores. I would go into a department store with an empty bag with a towel in the bottom of it. I would go in and take two of everything. I would try on the items, but would leave one on and take the other one off and act like that one didn't work. Then I would pack my bag up with clothes and go to the counter and say, "I purchased these items a while back and they didn't fit." They would then give me a store credit that I could actually buy things with. I had all of these different schemes and tricks going on. I would go as far as to give the stolen items to my parents as gifts for birthdays, Mother's Day and Christmas. One thing led to another, and it escalated from smoking two packs of cigarettes a day, Newport Shorts in a box to be exact. Then onto weed and from weed to mushrooms. I've done Sherm, I've done PCP. I've done hash. I've taken pills from ecstasy to Valium to Oxycontin. I tried anything that I could get my hands on that would get me high. I wasn't afraid.

The more and more I would rebel, the more my curiosity became stronger and stronger. Well, I must

And the Winner Is . . .

admit that I was a little afraid at first. I started off breaking the pills in half. Then I went from a half to a whole pill. When my body got immune to that, I moved up to two whole pills a day. If you know anything about ecstasy, then you're familiar with the saying "going on a ride or going on a trip." Ecstasy is a pill with a whole bunch of drugs compressed into one. You've got speed, acid and a lot of different drugs compressed down into this one pill. When you take it, you're going on this trip, as we used to call it, through the sensations of each of those drugs. You get hot then cold, then you're happy, then sad. It's over the top and very intense. I remember calling my mom one day from a club and it was the first time that I told her I was using Ex. I just had to get it out. I had to tell somebody. I said, "Mom, I'm high off ecstasy right now and I've been doing it for a while." She didn't flip out, but I could tell in her voice that she was hurt. She just talked to me. One thing I can say through this whole process is that my mother has loved me. She never shunned me. She never said, "You can't come out to my house. You can't spend the night at my house. You can't this. You can't that." She didn't enable me either. While I was around her, she did say something about God and something about me not doing what I was doing. She still showed me love. She still let me see that I was her daughter no matter what. She loved me and was going to tell me what was right.

And the Winner Is...

Everything that I was doing led to something else. It just kept getting worse and worse and worse. One time I remember going over to a friend's house on my birthday. I smoked ten blunts, and I took two ecstasy pills. This was the first time that I had taken two pills. I told my friend, "I'll be right back. I'm going to the bathroom." I got in the bathroom and I was stuck. My pill had already kicked in, and I was there for two hours None of my friends even came to see if I was okay. They had left. There was a whole new group of people there. In that moment I just knew, "Lord, You're all that I have." That was one instance.

Another instance was when I met a guy at a gas station. He looked like he had some money. He had a nice car. I left with him and we went to this island. We were drinking, drinking, drinking. I hadn't had anything to eat. I was smashed. I was sloppy drunk and passed out. The next thing that happened was when I woke up, I was lying on a bed, and I didn't know where I was. I opened my eyes and there were five men taking turns with me. They were gang-raping me. My whole focus was to make it out of the bed, make it out of the room. I even recognized one of the faces, a musician from the church. I knew this man's children. His children's mother was my friend. I just thought Jesus over and over in my mind. These men started to scatter like flies, like ants. They started hurrying

And the Winner Is . . .

up, putting their clothes on and the guy who brought me there said, "I have to get you out of here now." I got dressed and he dropped me off somewhere I didn't recognize. I couldn't tell anybody, couldn't even go to the police, didn't know this guy's name. I can't even remember exactly what I did after that.

I just suppressed it. I cried all night and I just medicated with drugs all night long. I will never forget that experience. I just wanted to make it out of that room alive. That's the state of mind that I was in. That's the kind of situation that drug abuse will get you into. These are the situations that promiscuity will get you into. These are the situations that rebellion will get you into.

I'm grateful to God just to be alive and to tell you the story.

Chapter Seven

Caught Up

While in high school, I actually fell in love with the weed man. We started talking and I fell for him. A classmate of mine and I would skip school to go buy drugs. When I say that I fell for him, I fell for him hard. This was the first guy that was giving me money. He was driving me in all of these different cars and taking me to all of these houses. The first day we met happened to be my birthday, so he took me shopping and bought me a new outfit and a pair of Versace glasses. I was on cloud nine. Then he completely turned me out. I would skip school every day. I would go to the drug house, trap house, weed house, a name you may know. I would go there, sit, and smoke weed all day when I was supposed to be in school. I ended up having 98 absences in my first hour class, the beginning of my senior year. My psychology teacher told me that if I would sing the last five minutes of class, he would pass me. Anyway, I was dating this guy, skipping school, and getting high. This guy had convinced me to start selling weed at school. I learned how to bag it up. I knew how to weigh it and everything. I would sell it and bring the money back to him.

And the Winner Is...

Remember in an earlier chapter I wrote about how I would disappear from home a lot? Well can you guess whom I was going to see all those times? Yup, you guessed right. My father had a friend who was a state trooper, so they ended up finding out where my boyfriend lived and began sending the police over there to come get me. The truancy officer came too; it was a big mess. They would call my boyfriend to see if I was there, and I would be sitting right next to him. They would say, "Is she over there?" He would reply, "No, I haven't seen her. She's not here." I would be sitting right there up under him and rolling up.

One time he sent me to the store around the corner and as I was pulling back up to the house, I could see police cars everywhere, and the police had them all laid out in handcuffs. I couldn't help but think what my parents would have done if I would had been arrested that day. So I kept driving straight as if I had no clue of who they were. The crazy part about all of this was that I was like a chameleon. Nobody knew I was a preacher's kid. Nobody knew my parents pastored a church or that I sang gospel music. I just adapted to every environment that I'd ever been in. At first I was quiet just to see who was who, what was going on, who the head was, who was calling the shots, who the weakest person was. Then I would work that room. I've always been like

And the Winner Is . . .

that. Always able to sit back, get my plan, and then work it. That's just how I was.

I was the first one at the club. I was the last one to shut the club down. I was dating this guy for almost a year and then I found out I was pregnant. I was 17-years old, in high school, on the basketball team, leading the gospel choir, and a part of the student council. College scouts were coming to the games to watch us play and I had gotten myself pregnant! I was leaving school every day because of morning sickness to the point where I had to drop out of school. My hopes for an athletic scholarship or even a music scholarship had all gone down the drain. I just had to walk away from it all.

It was just like a bad dream. All those years when I was just playing with fire, I was officially burnt. It was just a terrible time for me. I had this vision in my mind of what I wanted. I was going to get my life together. I was going to introduce my boyfriend to Christ. He was going to stop selling drugs. He was going to give his life to God. We were just going to be this happy couple and raise our family. That didn't happen. He got worse. I got worse. He started physically abusing me. One time he threw a glass bottle of applesauce at my head while I was holding our son. I was slapped several times, even in front of his mother. Now at this point, we were living together with his mother. I had already lived

And the Winner Is . . .

with his grandmother, then his aunt, and everybody in his family who had a house we could live in. I was miserable.

When my mother remarried, she married a man that had some money, so I went from driving BMWs to not even having a way to get to the doctor. I didn't even know how to use public transportation, so I really didn't know how I would get around. I wasn't prepared for any of this. This was not the life that I wanted for myself. Now I found myself 18-years old with a baby I couldn't afford to pay for or take care of. I was getting assistance from the state. I was at Focus Hope, stood in all these food lines–embarrassed, humiliated. And I had a family who was eating at the best restaurants, driving the best cars, wearing the best clothes, living in the best neighborhood and I had put myself into this poverty stricken situation. I hated myself for this. I couldn't keep my hair up and that really bothered me because I was used to getting my hair done every week. I was used to wearing nice clothes. My parents took very good care of us. My hair started falling out on the sides because I was very stressed out. I wasn't a good mother at all. I wasn't fit to be anybody's mother. I would leave my child for days at a time. I was making terrible decisions and I got myself caught up in this life that I thought I would never be able to get out of.

And the Winner Is...

It was a Tuesday afternoon and I was about four months pregnant at the time. I was living with my son's father but he wasn't there, and only a girl lived upstairs. She lived with her boyfriend too. We were roommates. She and I were smoking weed on this particular day, but of course, I wasn't supposed to be smoking—clearly I was pregnant. I would sneak and smoke because if my son's father knew I was smoking, that would cause a huge argument, so after we had finished smoking, I told her, "I'm going downstairs to take a nap." I remember watching Jerry Springer and lying on the bed. I dozed off to sleep and suddenly I woke up to her screaming from upstairs. When I ran to the stairs all I could see in front of me was smoke. She yelled, "Tasha, Tasha, Tasha wake up, wake up, wake up. " I got to the top of the stairs and called out, "Jodi, what's wrong? What happened? " She said, "The house is on fire! The house is on fire!" The weed tail had dropped behind the bed and started a fire. I was scrambling, trying to grab whatever I could to make it out of this house. I grabbed my purse, my boyfriend's money and his safe. I had one shoe on, a nightgown, and a bonnet on my head. I ran three doors down to a neighbor's house and watched through the window as the police and the fire department arrived, along with several news stations. They were removing pounds of marijuana from the house, so now I was terrified to go back down there—for obvious reasons. I didn't want to get in trouble and I didn't want to go to jail for something that wasn't mine. Not to mention that I didn't want the news people to get footage of me, because I didn't want my parents to see how I'd been living. I cried as I watched them bring

And the Winner Is . . .

out the dead body of our pit bull, Duchess. Looking back at it now, the enemy was trying to kill my son and me.

It was nothing but the grace of God that I made it out of that house.

And the Winner Is . . .

"A *day* is just a day *not* a century."
-Tasha *Page-Lockhart*

@tashapagelockhart

And the Winner Is . . .

Chapter Eight

The Trigger

Some years went by and I got engaged to my childhood sweetheart and best friend, who is now my husband. His name is Clifton Lockhart. We had met when we were children. Our parents were close and worked together in ministry.

At the time of our engagement, I was on and off drugs. Back and forth. I'd stop, I'd start, then stop and start again. We were living together, and it just got so bad to where I had different men picking me up from our home. Let me say this, no it's not right to cohabitate, it's not right to shack up (whatever term you want to use), it's not right. I don't believe in it. I'm being real with you and honest. However, we were living together. My parents were totally against it, but we had set a wedding date, and we were getting married really soon.

Then my grandmother died. She was my mom's mother. We used to call her Nanny. Nanny was my everything. Nanny taught me how to pray. She taught me the power of prayer, the power of reading the Word, and getting the Word down in me. She taught me how to cook, and she was there for me whenever I needed her. I think my

And the Winner Is...

grandmother and my great grandmother were a little churchy mixed with a little superstition. They'd say, "Don't put that umbrella up in the house and don't whistle and don't do this and don't do that." I think it was a little bit of both, but they taught us how to be women. They made everything from scratch. My grandmother used to make this magical lemon pie and I'm one of three people who have the recipe—my uncle Ollie, my Aunt Joan and I know how to make it. I would visit my grandmother in the nursing home and go up there to do her eyebrows. My grandmother always kept her makeup done. She was a hairstylist. She's the reason I love hair and makeup right now. My grandmother and my great grandmother owned a hair salon, so I grew up watching them do hair. I actually have my great grandmother's original cosmetology license. That was special to me. I'm the only one in the family that picked it up and actually pursued it.

My Nanny dying was a trigger for me. I was devastated. I felt like my world was getting ready to end. I had already lost my great grandmother when I was pregnant with my oldest son, Dshawn, in 2001. Now a few years later, my grandmother, my Grandma Nanny, was sick. It just happened so fast. We didn't even know she was sick. For a whole year she kept saying that she had a stomach virus. We all just kept saying "Well, nobody's going to have a

And the Winner Is...

stomach virus for a whole year. You need to go get checked out." I was at the house that day when her son, Uncle Ollie, made her go to the doctor. He forced her. He said, "You're going to the hospital." She went to the hospital and then that's when it all started. She found out that she had cancer, a bunch of tumors, and they suggested chemotherapy right away. One thing I thought was interesting is that she never lost her hair. It did start turning gray, however, but it never fell out. My grandmother's side of the family were Indian and Caucasian, so she had long hair down her back but would never wear it down. It would always be up in a bun and she would use this brown hair gel that would get on her ears.

She had enough faith for everybody else. She would sit up on the phone for hours and counsel and pray with people. My grandmother was a prayer warrior. If anybody in the family was admitted to the hospital, she would stay there with them. Sometimes she would walk the halls praying for patients on that floor. I watched her speak life into everyone else, so surely I just knew that she would rise up and overcome this disease. It was a trigger for me. I started using drugs all of the time then.

During this time, I was singing with my mom's group Witness. They were making a comeback after a five-year hiatus and so they asked me to join the

And the Winner Is...

group. I sang in a couple of groups. I would also fill in with my stepfather's group The Nation from time to time. At the time, I was a soprano which meant that I was singing in the rafters. So when Nanny left us, I just could not bring myself to sing or do anything anymore. I was so depressed. I started missing flights and big concerts. Of course, my parents were furious. I couldn't straddle the fence anymore. I couldn't be in church and still ignore what I was doing. I couldn't sing for God's people knowing my heart wasn't right. I just walked away all together.

I started singing R&B. I had teamed up with some guys in Detroit who had a studio and I started recording music there. I started writing from my pain and from my experiences. I started writing and wrote a whole album called *Feel Good Music* and it was packaged and was ready to go. We even did a remake of "Emotions." I was singing at every club in the city of Detroit. People knew me; I was extremely popular. I sang at all the casinos, sang on cruise ships. Anything you could do in the city, I did it. I sang everywhere. I saturated the city of Detroit.

I remember my mom having a conversation with me one time. She was so mad. This was before I was engaged. I remember she had found a flier. The whole time that I was engaged I was back and forth

And the Winner Is . . .

living at home. Clifton and I would get into it. I would go back home. I would come back to him. I was a mess and I was all over the place. Once when I was at home, she found a flier of me singing at a club. She said, "Your father is a pastor. We're trying to do ministry and we're trying to be a great example to the people and you are out there singing at clubs. You've got fliers and you've got your breasts all out. You dressed all provocatively. You need to choose what you want to do. You ain't going to be satisfied until you go on *American Idol* or something and just become famous. All you want to do is just be famous. Why don't you just go on American Idol?" I thought that was so funny. She just kept saying it. She was screaming at me.

I thought it was ironic that I would go on *Sunday Best* and win. It was still a competition, a singing show I had won after she said that. Anyway, it was crazy because after my grandmother died, I started singing R&B and was singing at the studio for a very well known R&B artist. I became his demo girl. I was doing demos for him and a lot of the major songs that were sent out to a lot of well known R&B pop artists had me singing the demo. I was writing music too. I was demoing the songs that they had written, and then they would send them out. Some of the songs got placed. Some of them didn't.

And the Winner Is...

I just got caught up in this lifestyle, seeing people around me snorting cocaine and. I started doing something that I said I would never do. I was deeply depressed. I didn't care about myself. I went days without cleaning. I would go days without doing my hair. I would go days without showering. I was a mess. I was a full-fledged drug addict, but I was a functional addict. I would binge, binge, binge and then I would clean myself up. I would get my hair done. I would put on some clean clothes. I would clean my house. I would show up at church on Sunday.

Nobody knew I was addicted to cocaine. One time I sat outside of a liquor store and left my four-year old baby boy at home by himself. I stood outside the liquor store, 5:30 in the morning. I knew the store was going to open at 6:00, so I left my son at home. I had to have a drink. I had been up all night snorting cocaine. I had to have a drink just to get up and make breakfast for him. He was going to wake up around 8:00 am. Because I had been snorting cocaine all day, I was getting ready to crash.

Whenever you come down off a binge and whenever you crash, you sleep for days. You may get up, eat a little bit of something, and go to the bathroom, then you go back to bed. But you sleep for days. I felt a crash coming on me. I had to get a drink just to stay awake. This is what you need to

And the Winner Is...

know about drug addiction. Most of the time a drug addict can't do just one thing. If you are on pills, some pills are uppers, some pills are downers. If you are on downers, you have to have something to keep you up. If you are on uppers, you have to take something or drink something that's going to bring you down. That's why I ended up smoking cigarettes, smoking weed, drinking, popping pills, and snorting cocaine. Without all of these, you will go into withdrawal—be very sick, feel like you're going to die. That's how bad it is. I had lost so much weight. Everybody knew me to be a very thick girl. I had lost a lot of weight but still didn't look like a drug addict. I knew how to mask it. I knew how to say, "Oh, I'm just on a diet. I'm just losing weight. I'm hustling right now. I don't have time to eat." I would say something funny like that, and when I came around, my hair was done. I smelled good. I was clean. I had nice clothes on. Nobody knew I was a drug addict.

It got so bad that my fiancé at the time left me. He said he couldn't enable me anymore. He could not stand to see me killing myself and abusing my body. So he left Detroit. He went to Atlanta and enrolled in college. We were separated and did not speak for two whole years.

Chapter Nine

He Used Me

I was always taught growing up as a kid that God is not going to use you if you're not living right. I truly believe to this day that in order to have an effective ministry, and any level of intimacy with God it requires you to surrender to Him completely. However, I'm a living testimony that there are people out here who will be used by God and don't live right. Here is an example of that.

I was always told that couldn't happen though. I had to experience it for myself to really understand it. Matthew 7:22 says, "Many will say to me and that day, Lord, Lord have we not prophesied in thy name? Then thy name has cast out devils and in thy name done many wonderful works? Then while I profess unto them I never knew you: depart from me ye that work iniquity." That Scripture would have been me, because although I was in the world, I was singing R&B, I wasn't singing gospel. I remember a time a lady walked up to me at the club in tears and she said, "Tasha, I don't know you. I just know you from here. I've been following you and I come here every week to hear you sing. There was something in your voice tonight. There was

And the Winner Is . . .

something about you. I don't know what it is, but it was like I found hope." None of these people at the club knew my background or knew about the church or knew about me being a PK or anything and she said, "I was going to leave this club and commit suicide." Oh my God. Lord, please. I was feeling bad about what I was doing. I couldn't believe that God would use me to save this lady's life—and I wasn't even singing gospel. I was singing something like Jill Scott, "Living My Life Like a Golden." Alicia Keys, "Unbreakable." Whatever it was, I wasn't singing gospel. I wasn't really even singing inspirational songs. I was singing straight R&B and pop.

In that moment God saw a need, a person who needed to be rescued, who needed to be saved and He used me. I was high as a kite off of ecstasy. The last thing on my mind was the kingdom agenda. The last thing on my mind was ministry.

In another instance, I was at a female strip club where I used to sing on the stage with the girls while they danced. It was in Detroit on 8 Mile Road and Hubble. I was a regular in there. One time a lot of the cash money crew were there. We were at a table popping bottles; we were doing our thing. One dancer came down and sat next to me. Instantly in that moment, I sobered up. The Holy Spirit began to speak out of me. I began to give out. I can't even

And the Winner Is...

remember to tell you everything I was saying. All I remember was something about..." five children and your boyfriend making you dance. You don't even want to do it."

It was a lot more than that. The young girl started to cry at the table. She put on her clothes and left the club. She told me, "Thank you so much. I needed to hear what you said. I needed to hear those words. God sent you to me," were her exact words. Again, I didn't have a kingdom agenda, but God used me in that moment.

Can God use a person who is not living right? Yes. God can do whatever He wants to do. Will God use a wino? Will God use a homeless person? Yes, He will in order to save somebody's life. God will go out of the way to reach one person. His will shall be done.

It's up to us to make the choice of not wanting to gain the whole world and lose our souls. I don't want to be out here making all this money, have all of this popularity, have a big stage, and die and then go to hell. It's up to us to embrace a life of righteousness and holiness. It can be done. It can!

I was living two lifestyles. I was singing praise and worship in church and in the world. I would go after church to light up a cigarette. I had a blunt tail in my purse in church, in plastic bag so it wouldn't

And the Winner Is . . .

reek or wouldn't smell throughout the whole sanctuary. I was up singing, frying chicken, serving on the Anniversary Committee, playing drums, working the sound. I was doing everything that I could do. Remember, I was a PK. Even though I was back and forth, my parents still allowed me to work when I was there. I'm glad that they did that. Some of you may say that's wrong. I was a functional drug addict, remember. I hid my life well. This was their way of reminding me of the purpose that was and still is in me.

They took on an approach of, " When you're here, you're going to work because this is who you are." Don't always be so quick to throw people away. Don't always be so quick to judge and to say, "They need to be silenced. They need to be sat down." That was my only lifeline. I thank my parents for loving me. I thank my parents for what they said every time I showed up after a long period, "Come on. Don't act brand new. Get in this choir. Get on those drums." If the drummer didn't show up, I was playing drums. If

And the Winner Is...

it were anniversary time, "We need you to get in the kitchen to fry some chicken." They immediately put me to work because they wanted to remind me of who I truly was. Not the identity that the world was trying to give me. Instead they declared, "You're not that person that you've become. This is who you are." I thank God for my parents every day for still pushing me, loving me and reminding me who I am and making me serve. I'm a servant right now to this day because of my parents.

They started their church when I was 14, so all throughout high school from 14 to 18, I was singing praise and worship, singing in the choir, leading songs. I was on the ministerial team. I started in ministry very early. Because of that, when I got pregnant, my stepfather who was the pastor, made me get up in front of the church and apologize to the church for getting pregnant. I didn't understand it at the time. I made sure that my opening statement was, "I didn't want to do it." Honestly I didn't want to do it because at that time, I didn't understand accountability, and so they sat me down and talked me through it. My mindset was that I had just smoked weed with some of these people here at the church. I knew some of them were having sex too. Some of these people sitting in those pews were gay. I knew this for sure. Why am I apologizing to them? At 17, I didn't understand that, but now as an adult I understand

And the Winner Is . . .

accountability. I understand because my dad trusted me with that platform, with that sacred desk, the pulpit. I had to be accountable to these people that I was standing before. I was screaming and hollering and saying Jesus Christ, yet when I left, I was having sex, smoking weed and drinking and then I got pregnant. What type of testimony or witness was I to the youth?

I understand accountability now. You have to be accountable for your actions. There are consequences when you rebel and when you go against the culture of the church, when you go against the kingdom agenda of delegated authority and what God has placed in order, our culture in the house of God. There are consequences to that. There is a way to help people reconcile back to Christ. I didn't understand any of that at that time. Now I do. I'm thankful for my parents for making me get up there and do that. Was I humiliated? Heck yes, I was humiliated. I was the pastor's daughter,, 17-years old and pregnant. I couldn't imagine what all of the youth that had been following me were thinking. I had younger siblings that I also let down. I'm just now gaining their respect back.

I'm grateful for that process now. I've matured to where I can say I'm grateful for what happened and

And the Winner Is...

I understand the importance of it now. It helped me and it molded me into the woman that I am today.

And the Winner Is . . .

> *EVERY SONG HAS A TRIAL CONNECTED TO IT.*
>
> @TASHAPAGELOCKHART

And the Winner Is...

Chapter Ten

Turning Point

Some people have to hit rock bottom. Everybody's rock bottom is different. Some go to jail; some end up getting pregnant; some end up losing custody of their children. I can't say what your rock bottom would be. I can't say what your turning point will be, but for me, while I was doing drugs and in my wilderness experience, my mother had been diagnosed a few years before that with rheumatoid arthritis.

As a result of my activity, she was so stressed out and worried about me that it flared up so badly that she could hardly walk. She had so much fluid on her ankles and her knees. She would have to get shots in her joints and would always have to have ice packs and ointments. It got really, really bad. Nobody knew that she had to ice her ankles and knees two or three hours before a performance. She was still singing and travelling the country. Nobody knew that the doctor told her back in 1999 that within the next ten years, she would be walking with a cane or walker. Nobody knew that she had this diagnosis. However, she was still pressing. She was still pushing. She was still doing ministry. She

And the Winner Is . . .

was still standing up in the kitchen with swollen ankles, cooking dinner for our family. I watched her go through this.

That was one of my turning points. One time I was gone for a long time. They were actually keeping my son for me. I wasn't a good mother. I wasn't around. My parents raised my son from birth to the first five years of his life. He was between my parents and his father's family. I came into my mother's house one day dressed nice, smelling good, making money. I was singing in places and feeling like I had it going on. My mother was in this white robe, and her eyes were red and almost swollen shut. Her ankles were swollen very badly. She was not getting around well. Just the sight of my mother like that did something to my heart. *You're killing your mother. You have to stop what you're doing. This is killing her. She's up all night worried about you. She's crying. She's stressed out.*

As a result of my lifestyle, her disease had flared up. My mother threatened, "Tasha, I will get custody of him. I will take him from you." I don't blame her. I was an unfit mother. I was never around. I didn't make sure that he had the things that he needed. Those two things were turning points in my life. It didn't make me stop right away, but I started thinking differently. I started processing stuff differently. I started downsizing. Okay, I'm was not

And the Winner Is...

going to do the cocaine, but I was still going to do the pills. Well, I was not going to do two pills. I was going to do one. I was not going ... That's not real deliverance. It twisted my heart seeing my mother like this. Having the possibility that my child could possibly be taken from me did something to me as a person as well. I started pulling back little by little. I decided not to disappear for two weeks but maybe for three days, then come right back. When I started downsizing, I started little by little doing things differently.

Those few things really helped me to change. My mother getting sick, my son not even recognizing me as a mother, not respecting me as a mother. He would go to my mom before he came to me. He would go to my sisters before he came to me. He would beg to go with his dad. He didn't even want to be with me. Feeling that rejection from my own flesh and blood was a turning point for me. It made me want to make some changes.

The last straw was when my fiancé left. He was someone that had been around all my life, my first love, my first boyfriend, the first person I told I was pregnant before I even told my son's father, before I even told my mother. He had a singing group and I took a road trip with him. We hadn't seen each other in a long time and I told him during that trip before I told anybody else.

And the Winner Is...

Then he walked away from me, moved to another state. We didn't talk for two years, which did something to me. It was another turning point. I'd lost my best friend with no access to him. no wishes for a happy birthday or a gift in the mail. Nothing. Nothing for two years. All of these things, these little things were turning points in my life, on the path toward my deliverance.

And the Winner Is...

Chapter Eleven

Get it Out

It had been two years of not speaking to my ex-fiancé, not seeing each other,. My mother had to sing in Atlanta and she called me from the venue talking through her teeth so that no one would hear her. She said, "Tasha, Cliff is here. He's here with a girl." I couldn't believe that he had brought his new girlfriend to see my mother's group perform. She put him on the phone and I lit into him. I was furious.

I had been living in this house with no furniture except an air mattress. Liquor bottles were lined up all over my mantle like trophies. No food was in my refrigerator. I had a four-year old son and I was still strung out on drugs. The thought of my ex-fiancé being with another woman broke my heart. Anyway, my mother put him on the phone and I said, "How dare you bring another woman to see my mother sing? I heard she wasn't even cute." I went off on him.

That's how we were sparked. That opened up communication between us again. We started talking on the phone. He asked for my number ,and

And the Winner Is . . .

called me one day and said, "I'm coming into town. I'm coming to visit. Can I come by to your house? What's your address?" Now this was the first time that I had allowed him to really see the *real me*. The whole time we were living together, I would leave the house and smoke. I would leave the house and drink. I would disappear for days at a time. I never wanted him to see me high because he was a church boy. This was my boyfriend from church and our families were in church. My situation was embarrassing, and I just didn't want him to see that side of me. This was the first time I said, "I'm going to let him see the real me." When he got there, I had a blunt lit and I was smoking weed. I was half dressed and I was drinking. I was doing everything in front of him. When I think about it, it was a cry for help because I knew I needed him. I wanted him to help me out of this. My parents didn't know what I was doing. Nobody in my family knew how bad it was.

He came and stayed at my house for two days and didn't judge me, didn't say anything. He just loved me and expressed his feelings, saying, "I want BET for you. I don't want this for you. You're worth more. You're worth more than this. There's more for you than this. God wants more for you."

He finally left. I hated to see him go. He invited me to come visit him for his birthday in Atlanta. He

And the Winner Is...

said, "I want you to come visit me in Atlanta. I want you to come spend just about two weeks." I gladly said okay. He bought the ticket in April and his birthday wasn't until June, so I totally forgot about going. The day came when it was time for me to go to Atlanta to visit him. I will never forget that day. A very close friend of mine begged me, "Tasha, you need to get on this plane." I said, "No, I can't do it." I started coming up with every excuse. I had been up all night snorting cocaine. My flight left at 7:00 in the morning, which meant that I had to be at the airport by at least 5:30. It was 3:00 am at this point.

I had been up for three days snorting cocaine. I was booted, I was tooted. I was whatever else you want to call it. I was completely wasted, twerkin', paranoid. I was walking back and forth to the door, to the window, to the door, to the window. If I heard something, I was crawling on the ground. I was just strung out to the point where if I saw a little white speck of anything on the ground, I was going to think that it was cocaine and I was going to try to snort it. That's how bad it was. My girlfriend said, "You've got to go. You've got to get out of here, Tash. You have to get out of here and I want to make sure that you go." I kept making excuses. I said, "Well, I don't have clean clothes." She said, "Take your dirty ones." Everybody needs a friend like this. "Well, I don't have any luggage." She then drove me to her house. Her mother was also a

And the Winner Is . . .

famous gospel singer. She took some of her mother's luggage, put my dirty clothes in it, took me to the airport, and dropped me off.

I'm so thankful for her having done that. I didn't want to go. They shouldn't have let me go on that flight. I was walking around that airport like a zombie. By the grace of God, I was able to get on the flight. I slept all the way there. When I got to Atlanta, Cliff met me. I could see in his face that he was looking at me wondering what I had done, Who was this person? He didn't verbalize it. I got in the car and slept all the way to his house and all that night. When I woke up, I found that this man had washed all my dirty clothes, bought me toiletries, new clothes. Everything was set up for me.

He took me to a church called New Life International Family Church, pastored by Bishop Jeronn C. Williams. My life has never been the same since. It was the first day of my deliverance process. After two weeks, it was time for me to go home. Instead, we ended up getting married. He looked at me and said, "Do you still love me?" I said, "Yes. " I said, "Do you still love me?" He said, "Yes" He then continued to say, "The Holy Spirit just told me that I need to marry you." We got the marriage license that day. A week later, we were standing in Marietta Park in Georgia getting married with a few friends, my aunt, and my cousin.

And the Winner Is . . .

We got married and stayed in Atlanta for three years. I was only supposed to be there for two weeks. I got on the worship team there and locked into ministry. I had accountability partners. This is huge. Hear me please. **Accountability partners,** people that held me accountable to the *Yes* that I gave to God. You have to humble yourself to have this type of system set up for your deliverance. This is the only way that you will get free. I didn't go into a twelve-step program. Although I'm not against counseling, I didn't have any. I didn't go to rehab. My rehab was prayer, worship, Word, and friends who loved me that held me accountable. They helped me strengthened my own will in order to stay free. I remember I would still go back and forth. I would do well for a while then two or three weeks later I would be back to smoking weed and cigarettes. I would buy a pack of cigarettes, smoke two or three out of it, throw the rest away. Two days later, I would buy another pack.

The Holy Spirit spoke to me and said not to throw this pack of cigarettes away. Put it in a Ziploc bag and put it on the side of your bed. That pack of cigarettes stayed on the side of my bed for six months and I didn't touch it. Then I was at the point where I put it up in the closet and kept it there for another six months. I didn't touch it. "Trust me, you can do this. I'm giving you the power." God would encourage me. The Bible even talks about the power

And the Winner Is . . .

that works in you. God said, "I've placed every tool, I've given you every weapon. I've given you the garment of praise for the spirit of heaviness. You don't have to be depressed. You don't have to be depressed about your past. Whenever you start feeling depressed, you start feeling down, start praising me. I've given you my word. I've given you my word to strengthen you, to empower you, to speak over your life, to shape your day, to frame your world. Speak those things and be not as though they were. I've given you a system for success. All you've got to do is use it."

I started working that system. I started speaking Word over my life. I started typing out words, Scriptures, printing them out, putting them all over my walls, my refrigerator. I was listening to the Word. I was speaking the Word. I was reading the Word. I was praying the Word. I was going on prayer revivals, praying every three hours. I was consecrating. I was fasting. I was tithing consistently. I was giving. I was doing everything that I could do to show God that I wanted him more than I wanted drugs or my own selfish desires.

This is what draws us away, the pride of life–the lust of the flesh, the lust of the eye. We're drawn away by our own lust. I pulled for God. "I want you. I want your power. I want your glory and I want it more than I want all this other stuff." There

And the Winner Is . . .

was one moment in my life when I was in Atlanta and we had a real strong deliverance service. I said, "Okay, today is going to be the day." I cried all the way home and I've always been the type of person who didn't want to be called out publically by the preacher. Instead, I drove myself home from church. I was with a friend of mine. Her name is Yvonne McDaniel and she's very significant in my life because we were on drugs together. When I moved to Atlanta and I got off drugs, I moved her down to Atlanta, saying to her, "You can do this." We walked each other through this practice and we got free together. We're still friends to this day.

So, we were in the car together and I was crying all the way home. Von is the type of person who is a prayer warrior, an intercessor. She saw me and began walking around the house praying right along with me. I was praying in the Spirit, crying, and weeping before God. I just began to scream out, "Get it out of me! I want it out of me now." I began to call out every evil spirit that was in me—rejection, perversion that was planted in me from the molestation, rebellion that had caused me to open up all of these demonic doors and caused me to walk in demonic activities. I had rebelled against God, his plan and purpose. I had rebelled against my parents.

And the Winner Is . . .

I began to call out all of these spirits. "Spirit of lesbianism, get out of me. Spirit of fear, get out of me." I said, "You dumb spirit, get out of me." When I say dumb spirit, I'm referring to the spirit that will make you stand in church with your mouth closed and not praise God. I would stand in church, so consumed with guilt and shame that I would not open my mouth. I wouldn't even say a word. That's called a dumb spirit. You have to call the spirits out by the root. Spirit of attention seeking, get out of me. I began to spit up and purge and the Lord was just dealing with me. Then after all of that was done and I was at a place where I felt lighter, I felt free. I felt like another person. I felt that even my countenance had changed. I could look in the mirror and see a different person. I know this to be true. I've seen it with my own eyes. Your look will change. Your skin will brighten. I know this for a fact. I changed. That day I made a new commitment to life.

After I had this experience with God, the Holy Spirit brought a Scripture to my remembrance, Matthew 12:43-45. It says, "When the unclean spirit is going out of a man, he walketh through dry places seeking rest and findeth none. Then he says I will return into my house from whence I came out. When he has come, he findeth it empty, swept and garnished. Then goeth he and taketh with himself seven other spirits more wicked than himself. They enter in and

And the Winner Is...

dwell there and the last state of that man is worse than the first. Even so shall it be also until this wicked generation."

I knew after this spirit was gone, I had to fill this temple, myself, with something. So if this spirit tried to come back, there wouldn't be any room because my temple would be full. This house would not go empty–this spirit would not return back here ever again. I asked the Lord to fill me with His Spirit all over again. I began to bind generational curses and I begin to loose freedom into the atmosphere. I begin to pray the Word of God. I began to say, "Spirit of love, consume me. Spirit of forgiveness, console me now. Spirit of intelligence...." All that stuff I had learned in school and had forgotten due to all those drugs that had wiped out my memory. I was a smart kid, but the drugs will do something to your mind and to your memory.

I began to say, "Spirit of intelligence crown my head with wisdom." I'm the head and not the tail. Spirit of poverty, leave me. Wealth, come into my hands. I began to call money from the north, south, east and the west. I begin to speak out everything that I believe that God is going to do in my life. I started writing it down. I started typing it up. Dreams and visions. He started giving me downloads of things that I was going to do.

And the Winner Is . . .

He told me I was going to be an entrepreneur. He told me I was going to be a millionaire. I was going to write plays. I was going to write movies. I was going to have a hair care product line. I was going to make records and I was going to win awards. I was going to do all these things that people told me I would never be able to do. I'm doing them right now because I believed. There is power in your tongue. Speak those things and be not as though they were.

Even if you're reading this book right now and you're not free and you want to be free, you can be free. You can be delivered. There is hope for you. Even if you feel like you're out of actions and don't know what you're going to do, there is one option. His name is Jesus Christ. It's the greatest decision you will ever make. I'm a living testimony that if you turn into the direction of God just a little bit, your whole entire life will change. Is there hard work that you've got to put in it? Yes. The day you give your life to Christ, will all of your problems be over? No. You're going to struggle, you're going to battle, you're going to war, but God will give you grace.

He will empower you with His Spirit. You will be able to endure and overcome every obstacle, every situation, and every storm, everything that could ever come into your path. God will empower you to

And the Winner Is...

overcome it all because greater is He that is in you than he that is in the world. The enemy will never win. You are a winner.

> "WE SERVE A GOD THAT'S COMMITTED TO CLEANING UP A MESS HE DIDN'T CREATE."
>
> @TASHAPAGELOCKHART

Chapter Twelve

I Forgive You

Some would think that after all that was said, after all that was done, after the deliverance that's taken place, that it's all peaches and cream, but that's when the real work begins. The real work begins after you say, "Yes, Lord." After you give Him your life. The enemy is not going to make it easy for you to be free. He's not going to make it easy for you at all. He's going to fight you even more. People started coming out of the woodwork, people that I had relationships with, people that had hurt me, and people that I had hurt. God purposely allowed me to cross paths with these people again. Some tests I failed. Others I passed. If I failed, He brought it right back around for me to test me again and then I passed it. I don't want to keep failing tests. I don't want to keep repeating cycles. God empowered me. He gave me strength and wisdom to keep moving forward, this is where the real work begins.

Everything that you need to be successful is already inside of you. You can do it, you have to forgive yourself first. Romans 8:1. "There is therefore now no condemnation to them which are in Christ Jesus,

And the Winner Is . . .

who walk not after the flesh, but after the Spirit." This Scripture is very important after your deliverance process and beginning your healing process because first you have to accept where you are. Accept that you put yourself here. Stop making excuses. Stop blaming others for where you are. Your life is all about choices. The Father gives us free will. We can choose to serve Him or not. You have the same choices that I had.

Stop blaming other people. This is a part of your deliverance and your healing . You have to take full ownership for where you are in your life. Whether it's you dropping out of school, getting on drugs, prostitution, becoming a lesbian or a homosexual, whatever the case may be, take ownership. You could be doing self-deprivation. You could be the type of person who hurts him/herself. You could be a cutter. You could be the abuser. You could be the one who is sexually molesting people. You could be the one who is raping, stealing, robbing. Whatever that is, take full ownership of what you've done, what you've become and where you are.

Ask God to forgive you and forgive yourself. True forgiveness is repentance and then you turn from that thing, that sin. You go in the other direction from the sin. True repentance is not. "I'm sorry. I'll never do it again," then next week or two weeks later you are back doing it. That's not real

And the Winner Is . . .

repentance. True repentance is, "I'm sorry. I'll never do it again. I will turn from this sin and I will go in the other direction." Repent, forgive yourself, forgive your accusers. Stop making excuses. Own it!

God will give you the strength to move forward. You don't have to live in guilt. You don't have to live in shame. Hold your head up high and walk in the purpose and in the plan that God has placed in you. If you are still breathing, and you are reading this, there is purpose for your life. Be obedient. In your obedience, there are so many benefits to living a righteous life. I'm living it now. I'm seeing the hand of God, the favor of God covering me like a shield on my family, and on me. There will be an open heaven over your life. All you have to do is say yes to God and operate in the power of forgiveness.

Whether you have to track someone down, whether you have to call or have a physical meeting, you also have to let people off the hook. You have to have mercy on them. You should have counsel from your leaders in your church or whoever is your spiritual adviser. Get wise counsel on how to handle this. It's necessary for your growth.

Some people resurfaced in my life. One of my accusers posted on Facebook, "So proud of you. Congratulations on winning *Sunday Best*." That almost set me back ten years when a memory of him

And the Winner Is . . .

molesting me as a nine-year old came back. I had to really pray and ask God for strength and He gave it to me. This person needed prayer and God and my forgiveness.

God, this is the moment right here where my faith has got to really come alive because I'm hurting. I thought I was free from this. Now all of these emotions and all of these feelings have returned, I'm 32-years old, and all of this stuff is resurfacing. My husband really helped me. He really talked with me, loved me, and walked me through this whole process.

You have to be okay with saying, "I release you. I forgive you. Even if you never talk or have a face-to-face conversation, I'm good."

You have to be okay and you have to be willing to forgive without the expectation of an apology in return. Everybody's not going to be where you are. Some people are in denial. Some people are in denial of where they were. The man who contacted me on Facebook had forgotten that he hurt me. He was in denial. I can't live my life in the bondage of waiting for an apology from someone who doesn't even want to face who they really are. All I can do is pray for this individual and us. What happened to me was a stepping stone to help free other women, help free other men, other young people going through the same thing.

And the Winner Is . . .

Give your pain a voice. Speak out. Tell somebody. Tell your pastor. Tell your mother. Tell your father. Tell your cousin. Tell your sister. Tell somebody what's going on with you.

To the parents, if you know something awful has happened in the family before, sit your children down, and tell them what happened. Make the devil a liar. Don't allow family secrets to create more and more generational curses and bondage in your children. Expose the devil. Be free in Jesus' name.

And the Winner Is . . .

Conclusion

I won *Sunday Best*, I won a Stellar Award, but not only did I win those things, I won the battle within **Tasha**. I won the battle with Tasha. I overcame me, my fears, my struggles, and my strongholds. I overcame, and I'm not a victim. I have the victory. I will not recreate my pain. I'm more than a conqueror through Jesus Christ. Because I said "Yes Lord," I have the tools and what it takes to help others gain their freedom. I'm a winner and so are you.

About the Author

Tasha Page-Lockhart

Hailing from the historical city of Detroit, Michigan, multi-talented vocalist Tasha Page-Lockhart, "Season Six" winner of *Sunday Best*, BET Network's hit gospel singing competition. Tasha is the daughter of legendary gospel singer Lisa Page Brooks of the female group Witness. She began singing at a young age recording commercial jingles for companies such as Chrysler, Bisquick, K-Mart, The Detroit Red Wings, and United Way, and in 2001, became the youngest member of her mother's award-winning group recording one album, *An Appointed Time*.

And the Winner Is . . .

Lockhart received a national recording contract with Kirk Franklin and became the first female artist signed to Fo Yo Soul Recordings/RCA Records. In 2014 Franklin released Tasha's debut album *Here Right Now* featuring the hit singles "Different" and "Faith Come Alive". Since the release of her album Tasha has remained a force in the music industry with electrifying performances on BET's *Celebration of Gospel, Bobby Jones, 106 & Park, TV One, The Stellar Awards* and countless other TV outlets. To support the release of the album, Tasha has toured House of Blues/Live Nation and McDonald's Inspiration Celebration Gospel Tour. In March of 2015 Tasha was awarded the Stellar Award for New Artist of The Year. She also won Female Vocalist of the Year in the UK for the Gospel Music Touch Awards. Tasha is a certified Life Coach and Founder of HartFelt Coaching Services. She is dedicated to helping others on their road to recovery and providing them with skills to live a healthier life.

Tasha is married to Clifton Lockhart and they have 2 children, Ronald & CJ. She serves faithfully as the Worship Leader at her parents' church, Restoration Fellowship Church International. Lockhart just completed a 20-city tour with Tyler Perry in which she lit up the stage each night starring in *Madea on The Run*. The play was filmed and can be purchased on DVD in stores and online everywhere.

And the Winner Is . . .

Lockhart says, "I want to inspire, encourage, and help people deal with everyday life, while leading them to Christ." She says, "It's that simple."

WE'RE ALL WINNERS

THE HOLY SPIRIT HAS GIVEN ME THE ABILITY TO ACCOMPLISH AND BECOME.

And the Winner Is . . .